CW01461147

LAWYER HUMOR HANDBOOK:

The Complete Tome of Lawyer Jokes, Stories, Amusing Transcripts, Puns, and Witticisms

Ronald H. Clark
Distinguished Practitioner in Residence
Seattle University College of Law

LAWYER HUMOR HANDBOOK

Copyright © 2023 Ronald H. Clark

All rights reserved.

No part of this book may be reproduced in any form—by microfilm, xerography, or otherwise—or incorporated into any information retrieval system without the written permission of the copyright owner, except for the use of brief quotations in a book review.

ISBN #9798862488678

TABLE OF CONTENTS

Preface . . . 6

Chapter 1 Q and A Lawyer Jokes . . .7

Chapter 2 Humorous Lawyer Stories . . .18

Chapter 3 Punchy Puns and Word Play . . . 34

Chapter 4 Law School Amusements . . . 40

Chapter 5 More Humorous Lawyer Stories . . . 44

Chapter 6 Amusing Transcripts . . . 55

Chapter 7 Witty One Liners . . . 73

Chapter 8 Laughable Legal Writing . . . 77

Chapter 9 Even More Humorous Lawyer Stories . . . 81

Chapter 10 One Final Humorous Lawyer Story . . . 101

About the Author . . . 102

This book and I am dedicated to my family

Nancy, Brady, Soojin, Malachi, Riley,
Clancy, Kara, Beatrice, Samuel
Colby, and Darren

And to all with a sense of humor—especially lawyers and judges

PREFACE

Yes, I've spent my adult life as a lawyer and law professor, and I believe that practicing law is engaging in a noble profession. Nonetheless, I do enjoy and laugh at lawyer jokes, humorous stories about lawyers' faux pas, law puns, and other such witticisms, and I want to pass them on to you. Humor can be an invaluable way to break the ice when giving a presentation. Amusing anecdotes can enliven any speech. Lawyer gaffes can serve as illustrations of mistakes to avoid when practicing law, such as suffering the backfire from asking a "Why" question on cross-examination. Lawyer jokes also show the human side of lawyers. Hope that you get some chuckles from this *Handbook* and pass the jests you like on to others unless they can't take a lawyer joke.

CHAPTER 1

Q and A LAWYER JOKES

Q: How many lawyer jokes are there, anyway?
A: Only three. The rest are true stories.

_____

Q: What do lawyers and bullfrogs have in common?
A: Both have a big head that consists mainly of mouth.

_____

Q: How does an attorney sleep?
A: Well, first he lies on one side, then he lies on the other.

_____

Q: What's the difference between a good lawyer and a bad lawyer?
A: A bad lawyer might let a case drag on for several years. A good lawyer knows how to make it last even longer.

_____

Q: What's the difference between a vacuum cleaner and a lawyer riding a motorcycle?
A: The vacuum cleaner has the dirt bag on the inside.

_____

Q: What do you call 25 skydiving lawyers?
A: Skeet.

_____

Q: What separates witnesses from the lowest form of life on earth?
A: The wooden partitions around the witness stand.

Q: What do you call 5000 dead lawyers at the bottom of the ocean?
A: A good start!

Q: How can you tell when a lawyer is lying?
A: His lips are moving.

Q: Why won't sharks attack lawyers?
A: Professional courtesy.

Q: What do you have when a lawyer is buried up to his neck in sand?
A: Not enough sand.

Q: Do you know how to save a drowning lawyer?
A1: Take your foot off his head.
A2: No.

Q: What is the definition of a shame (as in "that's a shame")?
A: When a busload of lawyers goes off a cliff.

Q: What is the definition of a "crying shame"?
A: There was an empty seat.

Q: What do you get when you cross the Godfather with a lawyer?
A: An offer you can't understand

Q. Why is it that many lawyers have broken noses?
A. From chasing parked ambulances.

Q. Where can you find a good lawyer?
A. In the cemetery

Q. What's the difference between a lawyer and a vampire?
A. A vampire only sucks blood at night.

Q. How many law professors does it take to change a light bulb?
A. Hell, you need 250 just to lobby for the research grant.

Q: If you see a lawyer on a bicycle, why don't you swerve to hit him?
A: It might be your bicycle.

Q: What do you call a smiling, courteous person at a bar association convention?
A: The caterer.

Q: What's the difference between a female lawyer and a Pitbull?
A: Lipstick.

Q: What do you call a lawyer with an IQ of 100?
A: Your Honor.
Q: What do you call a lawyer with an IQ of 50
A: Senator.

Q: What's the difference between an accountant and a lawyer?
A: Accountants know they're boring.

Q: What's the one thing that never works when it's fixed?
A: A jury.

Q: Why did God invent lawyers?
A: So that real estate agents would have someone to look down on.

Q: What' the difference between a lawyer and a boxing referee?
A: A boxing referee doesn't get paid more for a longer fight.

Q: What's the difference between a jellyfish and a lawyer?
A: One's a spineless, poisonous blob. The other is a form of sea life.

Q: What's the difference between a lawyer and a trampoline?
A: You take off your shoes before you jump on a trampoline.

Q: What's the difference between a lawyer and a leech?
A: After you die, a leech stops sucking your blood.

Q: What's the difference between a lawyer and God?
A: God doesn't think he's a lawyer.

Q: How can a pregnant woman tell that she's carrying a future lawyer?
A: She has an uncontrollable craving for bologna.

Q: How many lawyers does it take to screw in a light bulb?
A: Three. One to climb the ladder. One to shake it. And one to sue the ladder company.

Q: What are lawyers good for?
A: They make used car salesmen look good.

Q: What do dinosaurs and decent lawyers have in common?
A: They're both extinct.

Q: What do you call a lawyer gone bad.
A: Senator.

Q: What do you throw to a drowning lawyer?
A: His partners.

Q: What's brown and looks really good on a lawyer?
A: A Doberman.

Q: What's the difference between a lawyer and a liar?
A: The pronunciation.

Q: What's the difference between a lawyer and a vulture?
A: The lawyer gets frequent flyer miles.

Q: What's the difference between a mosquito and a lawyer?
A: One is a blood-sucking parasite, the other is an insect.

Q: Why did God make snakes just before lawyers?
A: To practice.

Q: What's the difference between a lawyer and a herd of buffalo?
A: The lawyer charges more.

Q: What's the difference between a tick and a lawyer?
A: The tick falls off when you are dead.

Q: What do you get when you cross a blonde and a lawyer?
A: I don't know. There are some things even a blonde won't do.

Q: Know how copper wire was invented?
A: Two lawyers were fighting over a penny.

Q: How can you tell when a lawyer is lying?
A: Their lips are moving.

Q: Why did New Jersey get all the toxic waste and California all the lawyers?
A: New Jersey got to pick first.

Q: Why don't lawyers go to the beach?
A: Cats keep trying to bury them.

Q: What do you call 5000 dead lawyers at the bottom of the ocean?
A: A good start!

Q: What's the difference between a dead skunk in the road and a dead lawyer in the road?
A: There are skid marks in front of the skunk.

Q: What's the difference between a lawyer and a bucket of manure?
A: The bucket.

Q: Why do they bury lawyers under 20 feet of dirt?
A: Because deep down, they're really good people.

Q: Why are lawyers like nuclear weapons?
A: If one side has one, the other side has to get one. Once launched, they cannot be recalled. When they land, both parties are devastated!

Q: What is the proper weight for an attorney?
A: About 3 pounds, . . . not counting the urn!

Q: Why don't lawyers play hide-and-seek?
A: Nobody will look for them.

Q: What's the difference between an accident, and a calamity?
A: An accident is when a bus full of lawyers plunges off the road, and into a river; a calamity is if they can swim.

Q: What do you call someone who watches a lawyer drown?
A: Lucky!

Q: What did the lawyer name his daughter?
A: Sue!

Q: Have you ever typed on a lawyer's computer?
A: Everything comes out in fine print!

Q: Why did the lawyer's chicken cross the road?
A: He had an easement.

Q: What do you get when someone is a lawyer and a librarian?
A: All of the information you need, but you won't understand most of it.

Q: How many lawyers does it take to change a lightbulb?
A: None, they'd rather keep their clients in the dark.

Q: What happened to the banker who went to law school?
A: Now she's a loan shark.

Q: What's the difference between a lawyer and a boxing referee?
A: A boxing referee doesn't get paid more for a longer fight.

Q: Why is it dangerous for a lawyer to walk onto a construction site?
A: Because the plumbers might connect the drain line to the wrong suer.

Q: Why is it so common for attorneys to be lost in thought?
A: Unfamiliar territory.

Q: What do honest lawyers and UFOs have in common?
A: You always hear about them, but you never see them.

Q: My wife accused me of being a terrible lawyer.
A: I couldn't defend myself.

Q: What do you call a lawyer who doesn't chase ambulances?
A: Retired.

Q; What's the difference between a cat and a lawyer?
A: One is an arrogant creature who will ignore you and treat you with contempt unless it can get something out of you. The other is a household pet.

Q: What do you call an honest lawyer?
A: An oxymoron.

Q: Why did the law student not win his case?
A: He had no conviction.

Q: What did the lawyer name his daughter?
A: Sue. And his son? Bill.

Q: What is the difference between speed humps and lawyers?
A: People slow down in their car when approaching speed humps.

Q: What would you prefer? A legal education or a Rolex?
A: Easy, a Rolex. It's cheaper!

Q: Why are lawyers good at limbo?
A: Because they always pass the bar.

Q: Why do lawyers make so much money?
A: I'll tell you as soon as I finish completing your bill for the punchline.

Q: What's the difference between a law firm and a circus?
A: At a circus, the clowns don't charge the public by the hour.

Q: Why is my lawyer a very smart guy?
A: He earns from my mistakes.

Q: What do law students need to make any event a success?

A: At least two parties.

Q: What does an attorney who works from home call his office?
A: His legal pad.

Q: Why don't lawyers play tag?
A: They know no one will chase them.

CHAPTER 2

HUMOROUS LAWYER STORIES

An attorney was working late one night in his office when, suddenly, Satan appeared before him. The Devil made him an offer. "I will make it so you win every case that you try for the rest of your life. Your clients will worship you, your colleagues will be in awe, and you will make enormous amounts of money. But, in return, you must give me your soul, your wife's soul, the souls of your children, your parents, grandparents, and those of all of your friends." The lawyer thought about it for a moment, then asked, "But what's the catch?"

———

A 50-year-old lawyer who had been practicing since he was 25 passed away and arrived at the Pearly Gates for judgment. The lawyer said to St. Peter, "There must be some mistake! I'm only 50 years old, that's far too young to die." St. Peter frowned and consulted his book. "That's funny, when we add up your billing records, you should be at least 83 by now!"

———

One day the phone rang at a law office and when the receptionist answered a man asked to speak to Mr. Dewey. "I'm sorry, sir," the receptionist said. "Mr. Dewey passed away yesterday." "Oh, is that right? Goodbye." But everyday for the next two weeks the same man called back, and the same exchange occurred. Finally, the receptionist said, "Sir, I have told you repeatedly that Mr. Dewey died, why do you keep calling and asking for him?" "Oh," the man replied, "I just like to hear it."

———

A man was sent to hell for his sins. As he was being led into the pits for an eternity of torment, he saw a lawyer passionately kissing a beautiful woman. "What a joke!" he said. "I have to roast in flames for all eternity and that lawyer gets to spend it with that beautiful woman." Satan jabbed the man with his pitchfork and snarled, "Who are you to question that woman's punishment?"

A man went to a lawyer and asked what his fee was. "$100 for three questions," answered the lawyer. "Isn't that a little steep?" said the man. "Yes," said the lawyer. "Now, what's your third question?"

A rabbi, a Hindu, and a lawyer are in a car that breaks down in the countryside one evening. They walk to a nearby farm and the farmer tells them it's too late for a tow truck, but he has only two extra beds and one of them will have to sleep in the barn. The Hindu says, "I'm humble, I'll sleep in the barn." But, minutes later he returns and knocks on the door and says, "There is a cow in the barn. It's against my beliefs to sleep in the same building as a cow." So, the rabbi says, "It's okay, I'll sleep in the barn." But soon, he is back knocking on the door as well, saying, "There is a pig in the barn, and I cannot shelter in a building with a pig." So, the lawyer is forced to sleep in the barn. Shortly, there is another knock on the door and the farmer sighs and answers it. It's the pig and the cow.

A young lawyer, defending a businessman in a lawsuit, feared he was losing the case and asked his senior partner if he should send a box of cigars to the judge to curry favor. The senior partner was horrified. "The judge is an honorable man," he said, "If you do that, I guarantee you'll lose the case!" Eventually, the judge ruled in the young lawyer's favor. "Aren't you glad you didn't send those cigars?" the senior partner asked. "Oh, I did send them," the younger lawyer replied. "I just enclosed my opponent's business card with them."

A housewife, an accountant and a lawyer were asked "How much is 2 plus 2?"

The housewife replies: "Four!".

The accountant says: "I think it's either 3 or 4. Let me run those figures through my spreadsheet one more time."

The lawyer pulls the drapes, dims the lights and asks in a hushed voice, "How much do you want it to be?"

A man went to a brain store to get some brain for dinner. He sees a sign remarking on the quality of professional brain offered at this particular brain store.

So, he asks the butcher, "How much for engineer's brain?"

"3 dollars an ounce."

"How much for doctor's brain?"

"4 dollars an ounce."

"How much for lawyer brain?"

"100 dollars an ounce."

"Why is lawyer brain so much more?"

"Do you know how many lawyers you need to kill to get one ounce of brain?"

A grade school teacher was asking students what their parents did for a living. "Tim, you be first," she said. "What does your mother do all day?" Tim stood up and proudly said, "She's a doctor."

"That's wonderful. How about you, Amie?"

Amie shyly stood up, scuffed her feet, and said, "My father is a mailman."

"Thank you, Amie," said the teacher. "What about your father, Billy?"

Billy proudly stood up and announced, "My daddy plays piano in a whorehouse."

The teacher was aghast and promptly changed the subject to geography. Later that day she went to Billy's house and rang the bell. Billy's father answered the door. The teacher explained what his son had said and demanded an explanation.

Billy's father said, "I'm actually an attorney. How can I explain a thing like that to a seven-year-old?"

A Dublin lawyer died in poverty and many barristers of the city subscribed to a fund for his funeral. The Lord Chief Justice of Orbury was asked to donate a shilling. "Only a shilling?" asked the Justice, "Only a shilling to bury an attorney? Here's a guinea; go and bury 20 more of them."

"How can I ever thank you?" gushed a woman to Clarence Darrow, after he had solved her legal troubles

"My dear woman," Darrow replied, "ever since the Phoenicians invented money there has been only one answer to that question."

The Pope and a lawyer find themselves together before the Pearly Gates. After a small quantum of time which was spent discussing their respective professions, ol' St. Peter shows up to usher them to their new Heavenly station. After passing out wings, harps, halos and such, St. Pete decides to show them to their new lodgings. Only a brief flight from the welcome, Pete brings them down on the front lawn (cloud-encrusted, natch) of a huge palatial estate with all sorts of lavish trappings. This, Pete announces, is where the lawyer will be spending eternity, (at least until the end of time..) "Hot Dang", the Pope says to His-self, "If he's getting a place like this, I can hardly wait to see my digs!". They take flight once again, and as Pete leads on, the landscape below begins to appear more and more mundane until they finally land on a street lined with Brownstone houses. Pete indicates the third walkup on the left as the Popes new domicile and turns to leave, wishing the pontiff his best. The Pope, in a mild state of astonishment, cries out "Hey Pete! What's the deal here? You put that lawyer-feller in a beautiful estate home and I, spiritual leader of terrafirma, end up with this dive?"

Pete looks at the pontiff amusedly and replies: "Look here old fellow, this street is practically encrusted with spiritual leaders from many times and religions. We're putting you here with them so you guys can get your dogma together. That other guy gets an estate, because he is the first (non-) damned lawyer to make it up here!!"

Carlson was charged with stealing a Mercedes Benz, and after a long trial, the jury acquitted him. Later that day Carlson came back to the judge who had presided at the hearing.

"Your honor," he said, "I wanna a warrant out for that dirty lawyer of mine."

"Why?" asked the judge. "He won your acquittal. What do you want to have him arrested for?"

"Well, your honor," replied Carlson, "I didn't have the money to pay his fee, so he went and took the car I stole."

A judge in a semi-small city was hearing a drunk-driving case and the defendant, who had both a record and a reputation for driving under the influence, demanded a jury trial. It was nearly 4 p.m. and getting a jury would take time, so the judge called a recess and went out in the hall looking to impanel anyone available for jury duty. He found a dozen lawyers in the main lobby and told them that they were a jury.

The lawyers thought this would be a novel experience and so followed the judge back to the courtroom. The trial was over in about 10 minutes, and it was very clear that the defendant was guilty. The jury went into the jury-room, the judge started getting ready to go home, and everyone waited.

After nearly three hours, the judge was totally out of patience and sent the bailiff into the jury-room to see what was holding up the verdict. When the bailiff returned, the judge said, "Well have they got a verdict yet?"

The bailiff shook his head and said, "Verdict? Hell, they're still doing nominating speeches for the foreman's position!"

A woman and her little girl were visiting the grave of the little girl's grandmother. On their way through the cemetery back to the car, the little girl asked, "Mommy, do they ever bury two people in the same grave?"

"Of course not, dear." replied the mother, "Why would you think that?

"The tombstone back there said 'Here lies a lawyer and an honest man.'"

These two guys, George and Harry, set out in a hot air balloon to cross the Atlantic Ocean. After 37 hours in the air, George says "Harry, we better lose some altitude so we can see where we are". Harry lets out some of the hot air in the balloon, and the balloon descends to below the cloud cover. George says, "I still can't tell where we are, let's ask that guy on the ground". So, Harry yells down to the man "Hey, could you tell us where we are?". And the man on the ground yells back "You're in a balloon, 100 feet up in the air." George turns to Harry and says, "That man must be a lawyer". And Harry says, "How can you tell?". George says, "Because the advice he gave us is 100% accurate, and totally useless."

That's the end of the joke, but if you are still worried about George and Harry: They end up in the drink and make the front page of the New York Times: "Balloonists Soaked by Lawyer".

––––––––––––––––––

The defendant who pleads their own case has a fool for a client, but at least there will be no problem with fee-splitting.

––––––––––––––––––

God decided to take the devil to court and settle their differences once and for all.

When Satan heard this, he laughed and said, "And where do you think you're going to find a lawyer?"

––––––––––––––––––

Santa Claus, the tooth fairy, an honest lawyer and an old drunk are walking down the street together when they simultaneously spot a hundred-dollar bill. Who gets it? The old drunk, of course, the other three are mythological creatures.

––––––––––––––––––

A lawyer named Strange was shopping for a tombstone. After he had made his selection, the stonecutter asked him what inscription he would like on it.

"Here lies an honest man and a lawyer," responded the lawyer.

"Sorry, but I can't do that," replied the stonecutter. "In this state, it's against the law to bury two people in the same grave. However, I could put 'here lies an honest lawyer'."

"But that won't let people know who it is," protested the lawyer.

"Certainly will," retorted the stonecutter. "People will read it and exclaim, "That's Strange!"

At a convention of biological scientists one researcher remarks to another, "Did you know that in our lab we have switched from mice to lawyers for our experiments?"

"Really?" the other replied, "Why did you switch?"

"Well, for three reasons. First, we found that lawyers are far more plentiful, second, the lab assistants don't get so attached to them, and thirdly there are some things even a rat won't do. However, sometimes it very hard to extrapolate our test results to human beings."

A certain lawyer was quite wealthy and had a summer house in the country, to which he retreated for several weeks of the year. Each summer, the lawyer would invite a different friend of his (no, that's not the punch line) to spend a week or two up at this place, which happened to be in a backwoods section of Maine.

On one particular occasion, he invited a Czechoslovakian friend to stay with him. The friend, eager to get a freebee off a lawyer, agreed. Well, they had a splendid time in the country - rising early and living in the great outdoors.

Early one morning, the lawyer and his Czechoslovakian companion went out to pick berries for their morning breakfast. As they went around the berry patch, gathering blueberries and raspberries in tremendous quantities, along came two huge bears - a male and a female. Well, the lawyer, seeing the two bears, immediately dashed for cover. His friend, though, wasn't so lucky, and the male bear reached him and swallowed him whole.

The lawyer ran back to his Mercedes, tore into town as fast has he could, and got the local backwoods sheriff. The sheriff grabbed his shotgun and dashed back to the berry patch with the lawyer. Sure enough, the two bears were still there.

"He's in THAT one!" cried the lawyer, pointing to the male, while visions of lawsuits from his friend's family danced in his head. He just had to save his friend.

The sheriff looked at the bears, and without batting an eye, leveled his gun, took careful aim, and SHOT THE FEMALE.

"Whatdya do that for!" exclaimed the lawyer, "I said he was in the other!"

"Exactly," replied the sheriff, "and would YOU believe a lawyer who told you that the Czech was in the Male?"

It had to happen sooner or later. Lawyer Dobbins was wheeled into the emergency room on a stretcher, rolling his head in agony. Doctor Green came over to see him. "Dobbins," he said, "What an honor. The last time I saw you was in court when you accused me of malpractice."

"Doc. Doc. My side is on fire. The pain is right here. What could it be?"

"How would I know? You told the jury I wasn't fit to be a doctor."

"I was only kidding, Doc. When you represent a client, you don't know what you're saying. Could I be passing a kidney stone?"

"Your diagnosis is as good as mine."

"What are you talking about?"

"When you questioned me on the stand you indicated you knew everything there was to know about the practice of medicine."

"Doc, I'm climbing the wall. Give me something."

"Let's say I give you something for a kidney stone and it turns out to be a gallstone. Who is going to pay for my court costs?"

"I'll sign a paper that I won't sue."

"Can I read to you from the transcript of the trial? Here it is:

> Lawyer Dobbins: 'Why were you so sure that my client had tennis elbow?'
>
> Dr. Green: 'I've treated hundreds of people with tennis elbow and I know it when I see it.'
>
> Dobbins: 'It never occurred to you my client could have an Excedrin headache?'
>
> Green: 'No, there were no signs of an Excedrin headache.'
>
> Dobbins: 'You and your ilk make me sick.' "

"Why are you reading that to me?"

"Because, Dobbins, since the trial I've lost confidence in making a diagnosis. A lady came in the other day limping ..."

"Please, Doc, I don't want to hear it now. Give me some Demerol."

"You said during the suit that I dispensed drugs like a drunken sailor. I've changed my ways, Dobbins. I don't prescribe drugs anymore."

27

"Then get me another doctor."

"There are no other doctors on duty. The reason I'm here is that after the malpractice suit the sheriff seized everything in my office. This is the only place that I can practice."

"If you give me something to relieve the pain I will personally appeal your case to a higher court."

"You know, Dobbins, I was sure that you were a prime candidate for a kidney stone."

"You can't tell a man is a candidate for a kidney stone just by looking at him."

"That's what you think, Dobbins. You had so much acid in you when you addressed the jury, I knew some of it eventually had to crystallize into stones. Remember on the third day when you called me the 'Butcher of Operating Room 6'? That afternoon I said to my wife, "That man is going to be in a lot of pain.' "

"Okay, Doc, you've had your ounce of flesh. Can I now have my ounce of Demerol?"

"I better check you out first."

"Don't check me out, just give the dope."

"But in court the first question you asked me was if I had examined the patient completely. It would be negligent of me if I didn't do it now. Do you mind getting up on the scale?"

"What for?"

"To find out your height. I have to be prepared in case I get sued and the lawyer asks me if I knew how tall you were."

"I'm not going to sue you."

"You say that now. But how can I be sure you won't file a suit after you pass the kidney stone?"

A Russian, a Cuban, an American and a lawyer are in a train.

The Russian takes a bottle of the best Vodka out of his pack; pours some into a glass, drinks it, and says: "In USSR, we have the best vodka of the world, nowhere in the world you can find Vodka as good as the one we produce in Ukraine. And we have so much of it, that we can just throw it away..." Saying that, he open the window and throw the rest of the bottle through it. All the others are quite impressed.

The Cuban takes a pack of Havanas, takes one of them, lights it and begins to smoke it saying: "In Cuba, we have the best cigars of the world: Havanas, nowhere in the world there is so many and so good cigars and we have so much of them, that we can just throw them away...". Saying that, he throws the pack of havanas thru the window. One more time, everybody is quite impressed.

At this time, the American just stands up, opens the window, and throws the lawyer through it...

A lawyer's dog, running about unleashed, beelines for a butcher shop and steals a roast. The butcher goes to lawyer's office and asks, "If a dog running unleashed steals a piece of meat from my store, do I have a right to demand payment for the meat from the dog's owner?" The lawyer answers, "Absolutely."

"Then you owe me $8.50. Your dog was loose and stole a roast from me today."

The lawyer, without a word, writes the butcher a check for $8.50 [attorneys don't carry cash -- it's too plebeian -- and the butcher hadn't brought the shop's credit card imprinter to the lawyer's office].

Several periods of time later -- it could be the next day but that would be unrealistic -- the butcher opens the mail and finds an envelope from the lawyer: $20 due for a consultation.

Q: How many lawyers does it take to change a light bulb?

A1: It only takes one lawyer to change your light bulb to his light bulb.

A2: You won't find a lawyer who can change a light bulb. Now, if you're looking for a lawyer to screw a light bulb...

A3: Whereas the party of the first part, also known as "lawyer", and the party of the second part, also known as "Light Bulb", do hereby and forthwith agree to a transaction wherein the party of the second part (Light Bulb) shall be removed from the current position as a result of failure to perform previously agreed upon duties, i.e., the lighting, elucidation, and otherwise illumination of the area ranging from the front (north) door, through the entryway, terminating at an area just inside the primary living area, demarcated by the beginning of the carpet, any spillover illumination being at the option of the party of the second part (Light Bulb) and not required by the aforementioned agreement between the parties.

The aforementioned removal transaction shall include, but not be limited to, the following steps:

1.) The party of the first part (Lawyer) shall, with or without elevation at his option, by means of a chair, stepstool, ladder or any other means of elevation, grasp the party of the second part (Light Bulb) and rotate the party of the second part (Light Bulb) in a counter-clockwise direction, this point being non-negotiable.

2.) Upon reaching a point where the party of the second part (Light Bulb) becomes separated from the party of the third part ("Receptacle"), the party of the first part (Lawyer) shall have the option of disposing of the party of the second part (Light Bulb) in a manner consistent with all applicable state, local and federal statutes.

3.) Once separation and disposal have been achieved, the party of the first part (Lawyer) shall have the option of beginning installation of the party of the fourth part ("New Light Bulb"). This installation shall occur in a manner consistent with the reverse of the procedures described in step one of this self-same document, being careful to note that the rotation should occur in a clockwise direction, this point also being non-negotiable.

NOTE: The above-described steps may be performed, at the option of the party of the first part (Lawyer), by any or all persons authorized by him, the objective being to produce the most possible revenue for the party of the fifth part, also known as "Partnership."

WASHINGTON STATE ATTORNEY SEASON AND BAG LIMITS

1300.01 GENERAL

1. Any person with a valid Washington State hunting license may harvest attorneys.

2. Taking of attorneys with traps or deadfalls is permitted. The use of currency as bait is prohibited.

3. Killing of attorneys with a vehicle is prohibited. If accidentally struck, remove dead attorney to roadside and proceed to nearest car wash.

4. It is unlawful to chase, herd, or harvest attorneys from a snow machine, helicopter, or aircraft.

5. It shall be unlawful to shout "whiplash", "ambulance", or "free Perrier" for the purpose of trapping attorneys.

6. It shall be unlawful to hunt attorneys within 100 yards of BMW dealerships.

7. It shall be unlawful to use cocaine, young boys, $100 bills, prostitutes, or vehicle accidents to attract attorneys.

8. It shall be unlawful to hunt attorneys within 200 yards of courtrooms, law libraries, whore houses, health spas, gay bars, ambulances, or hospitals.

9. If an attorney is elected to government office, it shall be a felony to hunt, trap, or possess it.

10. Stuffed or mounted attorneys must have a state health department inspection for AIDS, rabies, and vermin.

11. It shall be illegal for a hunter to disguise himself as a reporter, drug dealer, pimp, female legal clerk, sheep, accident victim, bookie, or tax accountant for the purpose of hunting attorneys.

BAG LIMITS

1. Yellow Bellied Sidewinder 2

2. Two-faced Tort Feasor 1

3. Back-stabbing Divorce Litigator 4

4. Small-breasted Ball Buster (Female only) 3

5. Big-mouthed Pub Gut 2

6. Honest Attorney EXTINCT

7. Cut-throat 2

8. Back-stabbing Whiner 2

9. Brown-nosed Judge Kisser 2

10. Silver-tongued Drug Defender $100 BOUNTY

11. Hairy-assed Civil Libertarian 7

The lawyer is standing at the gate to Heaven and St. Peter is listing the lawyer's sins:

1) Defending a large corporation in a pollution suit where he knew they were guilty.

2) Defending an obviously guilty murderer because the fee was high.

3) Overcharging fees to many clients.

4) Prosecuting an innocent woman because a scapegoat was needed in a controversial case.

And the list goes on for quite awhile.

CHAPTER 3

PUNCHY PUNS AND WORD PLAY

A family walked into a law firm to discuss the passing of a loved one. When asked about an *intestate,* someone pointed out the window at the highway nearby.

Q: What's a lawyer's favorite food?
A: Just-*ice.*

A lawyer walked into a sushi restaurant and ordered some "*sueyou.*"

Q: What did the judge say to the *battery* when he took the stand?
A: You're guilty as *charged.*

Q: Why did the elephant lawyer lose his case?
A: Because his argument was *irrele-phant.*

The golden retriever didn't make any money at his first law firm. He only worked on pro-*bono* -o cases.

The deaf lawyer didn't go to court because he lost his *hearing*.

The lawyer's client had to face a death sentence because of his bad *execution*.

When chickens graduate from law school, they become *legal tenders*.

Alligators make good lawyers because they are efficient *a-litigators*.

Children are not allowed into the bar examination because they're under-age.

What do poets always keep in their car to avoid paying legal fees to a lawyer?

A poetic *license*.

The lawyer had to move his cow because it got a *mooing* violation.

A photograph hurriedly rushed into his attorney's office and screamed, "I think someone is *framing me*!".

My father was a lawyer for 25 years before he went to culinary school. Now, he's a *sue chef*.

Early one winter's morn a lawyer walks out to his front lawn and experiences the *dew process*.

Q: How did the lawyer know that the knight wasn't the culprit?
A: He had an *iron-clad* alibi!

Q: Why wasn't the convicted law student able to go back to his apartment?
A: Because he didn't get *re-leased*.

A man learned that Congress authorizes a number of judgeships for each district. "Whoa! They get ships?" he said.

A debtor was told that she'd have to *liquidate* her assets. "Like, I have to blend everything up?" she asked.

A lawyer was discussing precedent with his client. He was presented with a "*per curiam*" brief. He asked, "What does *curry* have to do with this?"

A defendant told his lawyer that he wanted to represent himself "pro se." He said, "I'm very *pro say* . . . like the First Amendment and all that . . ."

A defendant was told that he was sentenced to probation. He seemed agreeable to this but asked, "I'm all for it, but what's '*bation*?' I should probably know if I'm going to be a supporter of it."

A judge indicated that she was going to make a decision *sua sponte*. The defendant leaned over and asked, "Is that what she's having for lunch or something? Sounds good."

A law student showed up to his tort class with a toaster. "Oh . . . I must have misheard . . ."

A client was advised that his claim was *unliquidated*. He said, "It was never liquid in the first place . . ."

A client showed up with a picture of his favorite rapper. When asked why he said, "Well, you said I had to prove I was *in-a-cent*. I figured 50 cent was even better!"

How do attorneys like their eggs? Overruled!

What's a lawyer's favorite part of a cooked turkey? The *suet*!

Q: What's a lawyer's favorite dance move?
A: "The Rockaway." They love to "*lien* back, *lien* back.

A defendant says that he won't speak to the police without the presence of his attorney. But after the lawyer walked in empty handed, he said, "Oh, no. I thought there were *presents* involved . . ."

I told my non-lawyer friend that I wanted a *settlement*. She said, "Oh! That's my favorite flavor of gum!"

I showed up to a client's office the other day, and the receptionist asked what was in my hand. When I responded it was an affidavit, she pointed me to man named David's office. I don't know why; I was looking for a Patricia.

A man mistook a courthouse for a hospital. When asked in the hallway what he was in for, he responded "a junk shin." He was confused when someone handed him a restraining order form.

When asked what *stare decisis* was, a girl in my class answered, "Um, a constellation or something?"

"I just agreed to be a power of attorney. I thought that meant I could just show up here and start working."

An attorney quickly realized that she could only discuss her cases outside of her house. Every time she said "pro bono" her dog went nuts.

After the judge announced that the attorneys would be conducting *voir dire*, a potential juror leaned over to another and said, "What is that? Like a fancy deer or something?"

CHAPTER 4

LAW SCHOOL AMUSEMENTS

The exam students have to take in order to apply for law school is called the LSAT. No, no. Contrary to popular belief, it doesn't stand for "Law School Admission Test." For simplicity's sake, it was shortened. It should have been LSATFNRBTSHNTDWLS: "Let's Study A Ton For No Reason Because This Stuff Has Nothing To Do With Law School."

"Oh, goody! Free legal advice" the dreaded phrase heard by every law student ever.

Every law student's favorite lullaby: "Twinkle, twinkle, little bar, how I wonder what you are. Up above the world so high, it's my entire future upon which you rely."

What do law students and marathon runners have in common? They both want to be first.

An art student arrived on the first day of painting class with an attorney and a piece of paper. She looked around at the wooden stands before everyone else, and said, "Oops! I thought we needed an *easement*."

Before students graduate law school, they should get vouchers to a chiropractor. Lord knows they're gonna need one after lugging around all those heavy books.

Kids in a third-grade class were going around the classroom and saying what they wanted to be. One little girl got confused as to when her time was up, so she asked, "A turn, me?" The poor thing grew up to be a corporate lawyer.

All new lawyers have arrived on the job and thought, "What the heck? The past three years did NOT prepare me for this!" at least once.

Why are there so many Irish lawyers? . . . they thought becoming a member of the bar was some kind of lifetime induction at their local pub.

This one isn't so much a joke as just an interesting fact. You know the traditional law school scene where the professor says, "Look to your right, next semester, one of you will be gone?" They ACTUALLY say that. Isn't that crazy?!

Every law student has heard, "Oh! It's wonderful to have a lawyer in the family."

Shirts that say "Harvard Law (just kidding)" are a favorite among the fathers of lawyers and law students alike.

Every law student has received a mug that reads "Trust me, I'm a lawyer (almost)" gifted to them at some point.

A law student was asked if he lifted weights. He looked down at his bulging biceps and said, "Nah. I've never even been to the gym. These are from carrying the books."

A law student was told that he was to use Westlaw to research his project. He spent the entire weekend watching John Wayne movies.

A law professor was confused when he was grading a student's paper that consistently mentioned Xzibit A, Xzibit B, etc.

A law student in class couldn't help but singing, "X to the Z and we all in the family" after the professor mentioned an exhibit.

Q: Where do vampires learn to suck blood? A: Law school.

The bar, in context of law, has nothing to do with alcohol. New 1L's can find this confusing at first.

CHAPTER 5

MORE HUMOROUS LAWYER STORIES

The lawyer objects and begins to argue his case. He admits all these things, but argues, "Wait, I've done some charity work in my life also." St. Peter looks in his book and says, "Yes, I see. Once you gave a quarter to a panhandler and once you gave an extra dime to the shoeshine boy, correct?" The lawyer gets a smug look on his face and replies, "Yes."

St. Peter turns to the angel next to him and says, "Give this guy 35 cents and tell him to go to hell."

When a lawyer tells his clients he has a sliding fee schedule what he means is that after he bills you it's financially hard to get back on your feet.

A man walked into a bar with his alligator and asked the bartender, "Do you serve lawyers here?".

"Sure do," replied the bartender.

"Good," said the man. "Give me a beer, and I'll have a lawyer for my 'gator."

There was the cartoon showing two people fighting over a cow. One was pulling the cow by the tail; the other was pulling on the horns. Underneath was a lawyer milking the cow.

A lawyer boarded an airplane in New Orleans with a box of frozen crabs and asked a stewardess to take care of them for him.

She took the box and promised to put it in the crew's refrigerator. He advised her that he was holding her personally responsible for them staying frozen, mentioning in a very haughty manner that he was a lawyer, and proceeded to rant at her about what would happen if she let them thaw out.

Needless to say, she was annoyed by his behavior. Shortly before landing in New York, she used the intercom to announce to the entire cabin, "Would the lawyer who gave me the crabs in New Orleans, please raise your hand."

Not one hand went up . . . . so she took them home and ate them.

Taking his seat in his chambers, the judge faced the opposing lawyers.

"So," he said, "I have been presented, by both of you, with a bribe."

Both lawyers squirmed uncomfortably. "You, attorney Leon, gave me $15,000. And you, attorney Campos, gave me $10,000."

The judge reached into his pocket and pulled out a check. He handed it to Leon. "Now then, I'm returning $5,000, and we're going to decide this case solely on its merits!"

Judge Bean and lawyer Bilgeworth were riding horses. They came upon an open stretch of country and noticed a hangman's noose dangling from a tree, solemnly waving in the breeze.

"Bilgeworth," said Judge Bean, "if that gallows had its due, where do you suppose you'd be?"

The lawyer looked at the noose. "Riding alone," he said.

The funeral procession included two hearses and a man walking a dog. Several hundred people followed the man. Curious, a pedestrian approached the man. "The first hearse carries my ex-wife's lawyer," the man explained. "My dog bit him and he died two days later. The second hearse has a lawyer who opposed me in some business litigation. He met the same fate."

The pedestrian thought for a moment, then asked, "Could I borrow your dog.?"

"Okay by me, but you're going to have to wait your turn like these other people."

A lawyer went duck hunting for the first time in Texas. He shot and dropped a bird, but it fell into a farmer's field on the other side of the fence. As the lawyer climbed over the fence, an elderly farmer drove up on his tractor and asked him what he was doing.

The litigator responded, "I shot a duck, it fell into this field, and now I'm going to retrieve it."

The old farmer replied, "This is my property, and you are not coming over here."

The indignant lawyer said, "I am one of the best trial attorneys in the U.S. and if you don't let me get that duck, I'll sue you and take everything you own."

The old farmer smiled and said, "Apparently, you don't know how we do things in Texas. We settle small disagreements like this with the Texas Three-Kick Rule."

The lawyer asked, "What is the Texas Three-Kick Rule?"

The Farmer replied, "Well, first I kick you three times and then you kick me three times, and so on, back and forth, until someone gives up." The attorney quickly thought about the proposed contest and decided that he could easily take the old codger. He agreed to abide by the local custom.

The old farmer slowly climbed down from the tractor and walked up to the city feller. His first kick planted the toe of his heavy work boot into the lawyer's groin and dropped him to his knees. His second kick nearly wiped the man's nose off his face. The lawyer was flat on his belly when the farmer's third kick to a kidney nearly caused him to give up.

The lawyer summoned every bit of his will and managed to get to his feet and said, "Okay, you old coot! Now, it's my turn!"

The old farmer smiled and said, "No, I give up. You can have the duck."

NASA was interviewing professionals to be sent to Mars. Only one could go and couldn't return to Earth.

The first applicant, an engineer, was asked how much he wanted to be paid for going. "A million dollars," he answered, "because I want to donate it to M.I.T."

The next applicant, a doctor, was asked the same question. He asked for $2 million. "I want to give a million to my family," he explained, "and leave the other million for the advancement of medical research."

The last applicant was a lawyer. When asked how much money he wanted, he whispered in the interviewer's ear, "Three million dollars."

"Why so much more than the others?" asked the interviewer.

The lawyer replied, "If you give me $3 million, I'll give you $1 million, I'll keep $1 million, and we'll send the engineer to Mars."

A farm hand consulted a lawyer. He had long tended the late farmer's cows, and believed they would be his when the farmer died. Now the farmer's son claimed ownership.

"I'll take your case," said the lawyer, "Don't worry about the cows."

The next day the farmer's son came in. The cows were raised on his land, he said, they should be his.

"I'll take your case," said the lawyer, "Don't worry about the cows."

Later, his secretary asked, "How can the cows belong to both?"

"Don't worry about the cows," the lawyer said. "The cows will be ours."

One afternoon a wealthy lawyer was riding in the back of his limousine when he saw two men eating grass by the roadside. He ordered his driver to stop, and he got out to investigate.

"Why are you eating grass?" he asked them.

"We don't have any money for food," the poor man replied.

"Oh, come along with me then," said the lawyer.

"But sir, I have a wife with six children," the second man answered.

"Bring them as well."

They all climbed into the limousine - no easy task - and one of the poor fellows said, "Sir, you are too kind. Thank you for taking all of us with you."

"No problem," said the lawyer, "The grass in my yard is about two feet tall."

The old man was critically ill. He called his lawyer. "I want to become a lawyer," he said. "How much for a quickie law degree?"

"About $50,000," the lawyer said, "But why bother?"

"That's my business. Get me the course."

Four days later the lawyer delivered the new law degree. Suddenly the old man was wracked with fits of coughing, and it was clear the end was near.

"Please, before it's too late," said the lawyer, "Tell me why you wanted a law degree now?"

As he breathed his last, the old man whispered, "One less lawyer."

A lawyer was filling out a job application when he came to the question, "Have you ever been arrested?" He answered, "No."

The next question, intended for applicants who had answered, "Yes," was "Why?" The lawyer answered it, "Never got caught."

A doctor vacationing on the Riviera met an old lawyer friend and asked him what he was doing there.

The lawyer replied, "Remember that lousy real estate I bought? Well, it caught fire, so here I am with the fire insurance proceeds. What are you doing here?"

The doctor replied, "Remember that lousy real estate I had in Mississippi? Well, the river overflowed, and here I am with the flood insurance proceeds."

The lawyer looked puzzled. "Gee," he asked, "How do you start a flood?"

An elderly patient needed a heart transplant and discussed his options with his doctor. The doctor said, "We have three possible donors; the first is a young, healthy athlete who died in an automobile accident, the second is a middle-aged businessman who never drank or smoked and who died flying his private jet. The 3rd is an attorney who died after practicing law for 30 years.
Which do you want?"

"I'll take the lawyer's heart," said the patient.

After a successful transplant, the doctor asked the patient why he had chosen the donor he did. "It was easy," said the patient, "I wanted a heart that hadn't been used."

A man walks into a friend and sees that his friend's car is total loss and covered with leaves, grass, branches, dirt and blood. He asks his friend, "What's happened to your car?"

"Well," the friend responds, "I ran into a lawyer."

"OK," says the man, "that explains the blood... But what about the leaves, the grass, the branches and the dirt?"

"Well, I had to chase him all through the park."

A group of terrorists burst into the conference room at the Ramada Hotel, where the American Bar Association was holding its Annual Convention. More than a hundred lawyers were taken as hostages. The terrorist leader announced that unless their demands were met, they would release one lawyer every hour.

A very successful lawyer parked his brand-new Lexus in front of the office, ready to show it off to his colleagues. As he got out, a truck came along, too close to the curb, and completely tore off the driver's door of the Lexus. The counselor immediately grabbed his cell phone, dialed 911, and it wasn't more than 5 minutes before a policeman pulled up.

Before the cop had a chance to ask any questions, the lawyer started screaming hysterically. His Lexus, which he had just picked up the day before, was now completely ruined and would never be the same, no matter how the body shop tried to make it new again.

After the lawyer finally wound down from his rant, the cop shook his head in disgust and disbelief. "I can't believe how materialistic you lawyers are," he said. "You are so focused on your possessions that you don't notice anything else."

"How can you say such a thing?" asked the lawyer.

The cop replied, "Didn't you know that your left arm is missing from the elbow down? It must have been torn off when the truck hit you."

"My God!" screamed the lawyer, "Where is my Rolex?"

Three lawyers and three engineers are traveling by train to a conference. At the station, the three lawyers each buy tickets and watch as the three engineers buy only a single ticket. "How are three people going to travel on only one ticket?" asked one of the three lawyers. "Watch and you'll see," answers one of the engineers. They all board the train. The lawyers take their respective seats but all three engineers cram into a restroom and close the door behind them. Shortly after the train departed, the conductor comes around collecting tickets. He knocks on the restroom door and says, "Ticket, please." The door opens just a crack and a single arm emerges with a ticket in hand. The conductor takes it and moves on. The lawyers saw this and agreed it was quite a clever idea.

So after the conference, the lawyers decide to copy the engineers on the return trip and save some money. When they get to the station, they buy a single ticket for the return trip. To their astonishment, the engineers don't buy a ticket at all. "How are you going to travel without a ticket," asks one perplexed lawyer. "Watch and you'll see," says one of the engineers.

When they board the train the three lawyers cram into a restroom and the three engineers cram into another one nearby. The train departs. Shortly afterward, one of the engineers leaves his restroom and walks over to the restroom where the lawyers are hiding. He knocks on the door and says, "Ticket, please."

A big-city lawyer was representing the railroad in a lawsuit filed by an old rancher. The rancher's prize bull was missing from the section through which the railroad passed. The rancher only wanted to be paid the fair value of the bull.

The case was scheduled to be tried before the justice of the peace in the back room of the general store. The city-slicker attorney for the railroad immediately cornered the rancher and tried to get him to settle out of court.

He did his best-selling job, and finally the rancher agreed to take half of what he was asking.

After the rancher had signed the release and took the check, the young lawyer couldn't resist gloating a little over his success, telling the rancher, "You are really a country hick, old man, but I put one over on you in there. I couldn't have won the case. The engineer was asleep and the fireman was in the caboose when the train went through your ranch that morning. I didn't have one witness to put on the stand. I bluffed you!"

The old rancher replied, "Well, I'll tell you young feller, I was a little worried about winning that case myself, because that durned bull came home this morning."

The Godfather, accompanied by his attorney, walks into a room to meet with his accountant. The Godfather asks the accountant, "Where's the three million bucks you embezzled from me?"

The accountant doesn't answer.

The Godfather asks again, "Where's the three million bucks you embezzled from me?"

The attorney interrupts, "Sir, the man is a deaf-mute and cannot understand you, but I can interpret for you."

The Godfather says, "well, ask him where the @#!* money is."

The attorney, using sign language, asks the accountant where the three million dollars is.

The accountant signs back, "I don't know what you're talking about."

The attorney interprets to the Godfather, " He doesn't know what you're talking about?"

The Godfather pulls out a pistol, puts it to the temple of the accountant, cocks the hammer and says, "Ask him again where the @#!* money is!"

The attorney signs to the accountant, "He wants to know where it is!"

The accountant signs back, "Okay! Okay! The money's hidden in a suitcase behind the shed in my backyard!"

The Godfather says, "Well, what did he say?"

The attorney interprets to the Godfather, "He says that you don't have the guts to pull the trigger."

Many years ago, a junior partner in a firm was sent to a far-away state to represent a long-term client accused of robbery. After days of trial, the case was won, the client acquitted and released. Excited about his success, the attorney telegraphed the firm: "Justice prevailed." The senior partner replied in haste: "Appeal immediately."

A gang of robbers broke into a lawyer's club by mistake. The old legal lions gave them a fight for their life and their money. The gang was very happy to escape.

"It ain't so bad," one crook noted. "We got $25 between us."

The boss screamed: "I warned you to stay clear of lawyers! We had $100 when we broke in!"

A guy walks into a post office one day to see a middle-aged, balding man standing at the counter methodically placing "Love" stamps on bright pink envelopes with hearts all over them. He then takes out a perfume bottle and starts spraying scent all over the envelopes.

His curiosity getting the better of him, he goes up to the balding man and asks him what he is doing. The man says "I'm sending out 1,000 Valentine cards signed, 'Guess who?'"

"But why?" asks the man.

"I'm a divorce lawyer," the man replies.

A young lady goes to see a lawyer regarding a minor matter. After consultation, the attorney notes the bill will be $100. She gives him a crisp $100 dollar bill and leaves. Sitting back, the lawyer gives the bill a flick and notices that the bill was so new and crisp it had another $100 dollar bill stuck to it. Now he was facing the age-old ethical dilemma, should he keep it himself or split it with his partner?

CHAPTER 6

AMUSING TRANSCRIPTS

Lawyer—Q: Doctor, before you performed the autopsy, did you check for a pulse?

A: No.

Q: Did you check for blood pressure?

A: No.

Q: Did you check for breathing?

A: No..

Q: So, then it is possible that the patient was alive when you began the autopsy?

A: No.

Q: How can you be so sure, Doctor?

A: Because his brain was sitting on my desk in a jar.

Q: I see, but could the patient have still been alive, nevertheless?

A: Yes, it is possible that he could have been alive and practicing law.

Witness: You mumbled on the first part of that and I couldn't understand what you were saying. Could you repeat the question?

Attorney: I mumbled, did I? Well, we'll just ask the court reporter to read back what I said. She didn't indicate any problem understanding what I said, so obviously she understood every word. We'll just have her read my question back and find out if there was any mumbling going on. Madam reporter, would you be so kind?

Court Reporter: Mumble, mumble, mumble, mumble, mumble.

Q: I show you Exhibit 3 and ask you if you recognize that picture?

A: That's me.

Q: Were you present when that picture was taken.

Accused, defending his own case—pro se--questions the victim of the purse snatch in a robbery case.

Defendant—Q: Did you get a good look at my face when I took your purse?

The defendant was found guilty and sentenced to ten years in prison.

Lawyer—Q: Now sir, I'm sure you are an intelligent and honest man--

A: Thank you. If I weren't under oath, I'd return the compliment.

Lawyer—Q: Doctor , how many of your autopsies have you performed on dead people?

A: All of them. The live ones put up too much of a fight.

Lawyer—Q: She had three children, right?

Witness—A: Yes.

Q: How many were boys?

A: None.

Q: Were there any girls?

A: Your Honor, I think I need a different attorney. Can I get a new attorney?

Lawyer—Q: How was your first marriage terminated?

Witness—A: By death..

Q: And by whose death was it terminated?

A: Take a guess.

Lawyer—Q: The youngest son, the 20-year-old, how old is he?

Witness—A: He's 20, much like your IQ.

Lawyer—Q: Now doctor, isn't it true that when a person dies in his sleep, he doesn't know about it until the next morning?

Witness—A: Did you actually pass the bar exam?

Lawyer—Q: Can you describe the individual?

Witness—A: He was about medium height and had a beard

Q: Was this a male or a female?

A: Unless the Circus was in town I'm going with male.

Lawyer—Q: Do you recall the time that you examined the body?

Witness—A: The autopsy started around 8:30 PM

Q: And Mr. Denton was dead at the time?

A: If not, he was by the time I finished.

Lawyer—Q: ALL your responses MUST be oral, OK? What school did you go to?

CHILD Witness—A: Oral.

Lawyer—Q: When he went, had you gone and had she, if she wanted to and were able, for the time being excluding all the restraints on her not to go, gone also, would he have brought you, meaning you and she, with him to the station?

OTHER LAWYER: Objection. That question should be taken out and shot.

Lawyer—Q: What happened then?

Witness—A: He told me, he says, "I have to kill you because you can identify me."

Q: Did he kill you?

A: No.

Lawyer—Q: Was that the same nose you broke as a child?

Witness—A: I only have one, you know.

Lawyer—Q: What was the first thing your husband said to you that morning?

Witness—A: He said, "Where am I, Cathy?"

Q: And why did that upset you?

A: My name is Susan!

Lawyer—Q: Can you describe what the person who attacked you looked like?

Witness—A: No. He was wearing a mask.

Q: What was he wearing under the mask?

A: Er...his face.

Lawyer—Q: Trooper, when you stopped the defendant, were your red and blue lights flashing?

Witness—A: Yes.

Q: Did the defendant say anything when she got out of her car?

A: Yes, sir.

Q: What did she say?

A: "What disco am I at?"

Lawyer—Q: Doctor, did you say he was shot in the woods?

Witness—A: No, I said he was shot in the lumbar region.

Lawyer—Q: This myasthenia gravis, does it affect your memory at all?

Witness—A: Yes.

Q: And in what ways does it affect your memory?

A: I forget.

Q: You forget? Can you give us an example of something you forgot?

Lawyer—Q: What gear were you in at the moment of the impact?

Witness—A: Gucci sweats and Reeboks.

Lawyer—Q: You say that the stairs went down to the basement?

Witness—A: Yes.

Q: And these stairs, did they go up also?

Lawyer—Q: Are you married?

Witness—A: No, I'm divorced.

Q: And what did your husband do before you divorced him?

A: A lot of things I didn't know about.

Lawyer—Q: What is your brother-in-law's name?

Witness—A: Borofkin.

Q: What's his first name?

A: I can't remember.

Q: He's been your brother-in-law for years, and you can't remember his first name?

A: No. I tell you, I'm too excited. (rising and pointing to his brother-in-law) Nathan, for heaven's sake, tell them your first name!

Lawyer—Q: How old is your son, the one living with you?

Witness—A: Thirty-eight or thirty-five, I can't remember which.

Q: How long has he lived with you?

A: Forty-five years.

Lawyer—Q: How far apart were the vehicles at the time of the collision?

Lawyer—Q: Were you acquainted with the deceased?

Witness—A: Yes sir.

Q: Before or after he died?

Lawyer—Q: Are you qualified to give a urine sample?

Witness—A: Are you qualified to ask that question?

Lawyer—Q: Did he pick the dog up by the ears?

Witness—A: No.

Q: What was he doing with the dog's ears?

A: Picking them up in the air.

Q: Where was the dog at this time?

A: Attached to the ears.

Lawyer—Q: You were there until the time you left, is that true?

Lawyer—Q: Did you ever stay all night with this man in New York?

Witness—A: I refuse to answer that question.

Q: Did you ever stay all night with this man in Chicago?

A: I refuse to answer that question.

Q: Did you ever stay all night with this man in Miami?

A: No.

Lawyer—Q: Have you lived in this town all your life?

Witness—A: Not yet.

Lawyer—Q: How many times have you committed suicide?

Witness—A: Four times.

Lawyer—Q: Were you alone or by yourself?

Lawyer—Q: What is your date of birth?

Witness—A: July 18th.

Q: What year?

A: Every year.

Lawyer—Q: Could you see him from where you were standing?

Witness—A: I could see his head.

Q: And where was his head?

A: Just above his shoulders.

Lawyer—Q: (realizing he was on the verge of asking a stupid question) Your Honor, I'd like to strike the next question.

Lawyer—Q: Can you tell us what was stolen from your house?

Witness—A: There was a rifle that belonged to my father that was stolen from the hall closet.

Q: Can you identify the rifle?

A: Yes. There was something written on the side of it.

Q: And what did the writing say?

A: "Winchester"!

Lawyer—Q: Do you have any children or anything of that kind?

Lawyer—Q: Mr. Slatery, you went on a rather elaborate honeymoon, didn't you?

Witness—A: I went to Europe, sir.

Q: And you took your new wife?

_____

Lawyer—Q: Officer, what led you to believe the defendant was under the influence?

Witness—A: Because he was argumentary, and he couldn't pronunciate his words.

_____

Lawyer—Q: Did you blow your horn or anything?

Witness—A: After the accident?

Q: Before the accident.

A: Sure, I played for ten years. I even went to school for it.

_____

Lawyer—Q: You don't know what it was, and you didn't know what it looked like, but can you describe it?

_____

Lawyer—Q: And you check your radar unit frequently?

Officer Witness—A: Yes, I do.

Q: And was your radar unit functioning correctly at the time you had the plaintiff on radar?

A: Yes, it was malfunctioning correctly.

Lawyer—Q: Is your appearance here this morning pursuant to a deposition notice which I sent to your attorney?

Witness—A: No, this is how I dress when I go to work.

Lawyer—Q: Do you drink when you're on duty?

Witness—A: I don't drink when I'm on duty, unless I come on duty drunk.

Lawyer—Q: So, you were gone until you returned?

In the middle of a robbery trial with a pro se defendant whom none of the witnesses could identify in the courtroom, the following happened:

Lawyer-Q. Look around the courtroom, Mr. Roubou, and tell the jury if you see the person that came into your store with a machete and robbed you.

A. Uh-huh. I don't — I don't remember the face. He was a regular customer in my store but —

Q. The person that robbed you was a regular customer in your store?

A. Yes.

Q. Look around the courtroom. Do you see that person?

A. What person?

Q. The person that came into your store with a machete and robbed you.

A. Yes.

Q. Could you point that person out for the record, where he's seated and what he's wearing?

A. I've seen him in my store before, this guy right here.

Q. For the record, you just pointed to the court reporter.

THE COURT: I know you're good, Mr. Reporter, but can you work that little machine in handcuffs?

Lawyer-Q. Do you feel you have a pretty good memory about things?

A. Sometimes he does.

Q. I'm asking about you, ma'am.

A. Me?

Q. Yes, ma'am.

A. Yeah. I ain't crazy. I may be old, but I ain't crazy.

Q. All right. Let's talk about motherhood. Do you value it as an institution?

A. Do I value motherhood?

Q. Yes, sir. As an economist.

A. I'm in favor of it.

Q. Is there anything that would refresh your recollection as to whether or not you were experiencing any pain at the scene?

A. A better memory.

Lawyer-Q. Do you know how many beds the University of Tennessee hospital has?

A. Hundreds, but I couldn't tell you.

Q. How many hospitals are in Knoxville?

A. Probably about 14. No, probably about 10.

Q. Do you know the population of — of Knoxville?

A. Metropolitan area probably has about 750,000.

Q. Do you know the team colors of the University of Tennessee football team?

A. No. I know the — I know the Rocky Top song, though. Orange and white.

Prosecutor-Q: How fast was the car coming toward you?
A: I am not a thermometer, so I can't tell you the speed limit.

Attorney- Q: What did the doctor tell you was the condition of the body when he performed the autopsy?
Medical Examiner Witness-A: He described it as dead.

Prosecutor-Q: Do you see the defendant in court today?
A: Yes, I do.
Q: How is he dressed?
A: He looks pretty sharp.

Prosecutor (addressing the court): The People have evidence that the life of the witness is in jeopardy, and it is reasonable to apprehend he will not be able to attend the trial if he is not alive at that time.

Lawyer-Q: Were you involved in a romantic relationship with her?
A: I ain't involved in no romantic relationship with her. I'm married to her.

This from the Texas Bar Journal (from a trial transcript):

The Court: Next witness.

Ms. Olschner: Your honor, at this time, I would like to swat Mr. Buck in the head with his client's deposition.

The Court: You mean read it?

Ms. Olschner: No sir, I mean swat him in the head with it. Pursuant to Rule 32, I may use this deposition for any purpose, and that is the purpose for which I want to use it.

The Court: Well, it does say that. (pause) There being no objection, you may proceed.

Ms. Olschner: Thank you, Judge Hanes. (whereupon Ms. Olschner swatted Mr. Buck in the head with the deposition.)

Mr. Buck: But, Judge.

The Court: Next witness.

Mr. Buck: We object.

The Court: Sustained. Next witness.

Federal Rule of Civil Procedure 32(3) Deposition of Party, Agent, or Designee. An adverse party may use for any purpose the deposition of a party or anyone who, when deposed, was the party's officer, director, managing agent, or designee under Rule 30(b)(6) or 31(a)(4).

Defense attorney-Q: You indicated at the time you seized it, it had a damage to the dashboard?

A: That is correct.

Q: And one of the windows?

A: That's correct.

Q: Do you yourself know what happened?

Prosecutor: Again, I believe that is an area - he is going into an area you already ruled upon.

Defense counsel: The last time they had it, it got damaged.

Judge: Have you heard the words of magic, Have you, Virgil?

Court Reporter: No, I haven't.

Prosecutor: You mean, I should say "I object"?

Judge: That's the one.

Prosecutor: Excuse me.

Judge: That brings the rubber duck down.

Prosecutor: Objection.

Judge: Sustained.

Lawyer-Q: Did you observe anything?

A: Yes, we did. When we found the vehicle, we saw several unusual items in the car in the right front floorboard of the vehicle. There was what appeared to be a Molotov cocktail, a green bottle--

Opposing Counsel: Objection. I'm going to object to the word. "Molotov cocktail".

Judge: What is your objection, Counsel?

Opposing Counsel. It's inflammatory, Your Honor.

Making a Record in the Transcript and Making an Objection: When you know it's wrong, but you just can't come up with the grounds for the objection, here is what a lawyer should say according to some of the leading experts in trial work:

JACK CURTAIN, Boston, Massachusetts: He's getting close to that legal problem, Your Honor.

JOHN KAPLAN, Stanford Law School: That's unfair, Your Honor!

JON WALTZ, Northwestern University of Law School: That's unfair, Your Honor, and he knows it.

BOB HANLEY: Denver, Colorado (In response to protracted leading question): I've been listening to Mr. McNamara for half an hour, Your Honor, and if he persists in testifying, I'll have no alternative but to mark him and offer him in evidence.

FAUST ROSSI, Cornell Law School: Incompetent, irrelevant, and immaterial, and against the interests of justice, and just no good.

IRVING YOUNGER, University of Minnesota School of Law: He's getting on dangerous ground, Your Honor.

TOM MCNAMARA, Grand Rapids, Michigan: Objection, Your Honor. Counsel knows that's totally improper.

TIM BROSNAHAN, San Francisco, California: Judge, could we get on with something that had to do with this case?

HAMILTON BURGER: Perry Mason's traditional opponent: Objection, Your Honor, that's highly unusual.

A defense attorney was cross examining a police officer during a felony trial. It went like this:

Q: Officer, Did you see my client fleeing the scene?

A: No Sir, but I subsequently observed a person matching the description of the offender running several blocks away.

Q: Officer, who provided this description?

A: The officer who responded to the scene.

Q: a fellow officer provided the description of this so-called offender. Do you trust your fellow officers?

A: Yes, Sir, with my life.

Q: WITH YOUR LIFE? Let me ask you this then. Officer - do you have a locker room in the police station - a room where you change your clothes in preparation for your daily duties?

A: Yes Sir, we do.

Q: And do you have a locker in that room?

A Yes, Sir, I do.

Q: And, do you have a lock on your locker?

A: Yes, Sir.

Q: Now why is it, officer, IF YOU TRUST YOUR FELLOW OFFICERS WITH YOUR LIFE, that you find it necessary to lock your locker in a room that you share with the officers?

A: You see, sir, we share the building with a court complex, and sometimes defense attorneys have been known to walk through that room.

CHAPTER 7

WITTY ONE LINERS

If an apple a day keeps the doctor away, how many orchards does it take to keep a lawyer away?

The defendant who pleads their own case has a fool for a client, but at least there will be no problem with fee-splitting.

When a lawyer tells his clients he has a sliding fee schedule what he means is that after he bills you it's financially hard to get back on your feet.

It was so cold last winter that I saw a lawyer with his hands in his own pockets.

If you laid all of the lawyers in the world, end to end, on the equator, it would be a good idea to just leave them there.

I don't know about that revolutionary hero guy, but if I had but one life to give for my country, it would be a lawyer's.

Did you hear about the lawyer whose firm had so few clients that he divorced his wife just so he would have a case?

There's an interesting new novel about two ex-convicts. One of them studies to become a lawyer, the other decides to go straight.

"A lawyer is a gentleman who rescues your estate from your enemies and keeps it for himself." —*Lord Brougham*

"It is interesting to note that criminals have multiplied of late, and lawyers have also; but I repeat myself." –Mark Twain

A jury is a collection of people banded together to decide who hired the better lawyer.

When an attorney gets married, she says "I accept the terms and conditions."

Lawyers will wish you a happy holiday but remind you they can in no way guarantee it.

If a lawyer works on a case in the forest and no one is around to hear it, can he still bill his time?

Forget seven years for breaking a mirror because a lawyer might be able to get you down to five.

A man hired a lawyer to sue the airline for losing his baggage, but unfortunately, he lost the case.

When you tell lawyers you love them, they ask for evidence to support your statement.

Did you hear they just released a new Barbie doll called "Divorced Barbie" –it comes with half of Ken's things and alimony.

Don't judge a law book by its cover-up.

"Criminal Lawyer" is redundant.

Talk is cheap until you hire a lawyer.

I sought out a divorce attorney named Rich—I thought it would be a good omen for my financial status after the proceedings were over.

Lawsuits—a lawyer's favorite outfit.

Lawyers play DJ Khaled's "All I do is Win" in their heads before entering a courtroom.

Family lawyer—more like gossip funnel, best friend, and therapist.

When a lawyer reads a death notice, the first thing he wonders is, "Did they have a will?"

CHAPTER 8

LAUGHABLE LEGAL WRITING

Law schools should focus on producing professional communicators—lawyers—who are effective writers. However, Bryan A. Garner in his column for the ABA Journal titled, "Why Lawyers Can't Write" with the subtitle: "Science has something to do with it, and law schools are partly to blame." stated:

> While lawyers are the most highly paid rhetoricians in the world, we're among the most inept wielders of words. Stop and think about that. The blame goes primarily to law schools. They inundate students with poorly written, legalese-riddled opinions that read like over-the-top Marx Brothers parodies of stiffness and hyperformality. And they offer law students little if any feedback (on substance, much less style) from professors on exams and writing assignments. (ABA Journal, March 2013, p. 24)

Garner was echoing the theme of Jim McElhaney, advocacy instructor and ABA Journal contributor for 25 years, who wrote this in a September 2012 ABA Journal article:

> Law school is as much obscure vocabulary training as it is legal reasoning. At its best, it can teach close thought and precise expression. But too often law school is reverse Hogwarts – where Harry Potter trained to be a wizard – that secretly implants into its students the power to confuse other people instead of sowing the magic seeds of clarity and simplicity.
>
> So we lard our speech and writing with words and phrases of awkward obscurity and rarely have anything to do with legal precision but that unmistakably say,

'This was written – or said – by a lawyer.'

Because we are professional communicators, it is our obligation to be plain and simple. It's not our readers' and listeners' jobs to try to understand us. It's our job to make certain that everything we write and say commands instant   comprehension.

And because we weren't turned out that way by our law school training, we have to reprogram ourselves if we want to be effective communicators.

One day in contract law class, the professor asked one of his better students, "Now if you were to give someone an orange, how would you go about it?"

The student replied, "I'd write a contract that says, 'Here's an orange.'"

The professor was livid. "No! No! Think like a lawyer!"

The student then responded, "Okay, I'd write, 'I hereby give and convey to you all and singular, my estate and interests, rights, claim, title, claim and advantages of and in, said orange, together with all its rind, juice, pulp, and seeds, and all rights and advantages with full power to bite, cut, freeze and otherwise eat, the same, or give the same away with and without the pulp, juice, rind and seeds, anything herein before or hereinafter or in any deed, or deeds, instruments of whatever nature or kind whatsoever to the contrary in anywise notwithstanding...'"

Here is an example of witty writing—in a pretrial ruling on a motion for a more definite statement in a complaint, the Honorable Ronald B. Leighton, United States District Judge, Western District of Washington at Tacoma, Washington provided gems of judicial humor when discussing a pleading. In *Presidio Group, LLC, vs. GMAC Mortgage, LLC*. Judge Leighton's order granting the motion began with William Shakespeare, Hamlet, Act 2, Scene 2, Line 90: "Brevity is the soul of wit."

The good Judge then went on to point out that "(b)revity is also the soul of a pleading. See Fed. R. Civ. P. 8(a). The Federal Rules envision a "short and plain statement of the claim showing that the pleader is entitled to relief." He then described portions of the 465-page Complaint:

> Not before page 30 does the Complaint address the facts alleged. Plaintiff's allegations continue for 87 pages – including a 37-page pit-stop to quote e-mails. (Compl. 39-76). The Court notes, with some irony, that in his response opposing Defendants' motions for a more definite statement, the Plaintiff successfully states his allegations in two pages.

Then, in granting the motion, Judge Leighton added a bit of his own poetry:

> Plaintiff has a great deal to say
> But it seems he skipped Rule 8(a),
> His Complaint is too long,
> Which renders it wrong,
> Please re-write and re-file today.

To assist lawyers, Sally Bulford, a Utah prosecutor, provided these witty writing pointers for lawyers under the title "How to Write Good":

1. Avoid alliteration. Always.

2. Prepositions are not words to end sentences with.

3. Avoid cliches like the plague. (They're old hat.)

4. Employ the vernacular.

5. Eschew ampersands & abbreviations, etc.

6. Parenthetical remarks (however relevant) are unnecessary.

7. It is wrong to ever split an infinitive.

8. Contractions aren't necessary.

9. Foreign words and phrases are not apropos.

10. One should never generalize.

11. Eliminate quotations. As Ralph Waldo Emerson said, "I hate quotations. Tell me what you know."

12. Comparisons are as bad as clichés.

13. Don't be redundant; don't use more words than necessary; it's highly superfluous.

14. Be more or less specific.

15. Understatement is always best.

16. One-word sentences? Eliminate.

17. Analogies in writing are like feathers on a snake.

18. The passive voice is to be avoided.

19. Go around the barn at high noon to avoid colloquialisms.

20. Even if a mixed metaphor sings, it should be derailed.

21. Who needs rhetorical questions?

22. Exaggeration is a billion times worse than understatement.

CHAPTER 9

EVEN MORE HUMOROUS LAWYER STORIES

A truck driver used to amuse himself by running over lawyers he would see walking down the side of the road. Every time he would see a lawyer walking along the road, he would swerve to hit him. There would be a loud "THUMP" and then he would swerve back on the road. One day, as the truck driver was driving along, he saw a priest hitchhiking. He thought he would do a good turn and pulled the truck over. He asked the priest, "Where are you going, Father?" "I'm going to the church five miles down the road," replied the priest. "No problem, Father! I'll give you a lift. Climb in the truck." The happy priest climbed into the passenger seat and the truck driver continued down the road.

Suddenly the truck driver saw a lawyer walking down the road, and instinctively he swerved to hit him. But then he remembered there was a priest in the truck with him, so at the last minute he swerved back to the road, narrowly missing the lawyer. However, even though he was certain he had missed the lawyer, he still heard a loud "THUMP." Not understanding where the noise came from, he glanced in his mirrors. When he didn't see anything, he turned to the priest and said, "I'm sorry Father. I almost hit that lawyer." "That's okay my son," replied the priest. "I got him with the door!"

Five surgeons were taking a coffee break and discussing their work.

The first said, "I think accountants are the easiest to operate on; you open them up and everything inside is numbered."

The second said, "I think librarians are the easiest to operate on; you open them up and everything inside is in alphabetical order."

The third said, "I like to operate on electricians; you open them up and everything inside is color-coded."

The fourth surgeon said, "I like Engineers...they always understand when you have a few parts left over at the end..."

The fifth one said, "I like to operate on lawyers; they're heartless, spineless, gutless, and their heads and their butts are interchangeable."

A woman shot her husband dead. A preacher who saw the shooting asked, "Woman, why did you shoot your husband?" "Because he was a lawyer and an evil man. He was going to move to Anchorage!" "Woman," said the man of the cloth, "You cannot stop a lawyer from going to Anchorage by shooting him."

The local United Way office realized that it had never received a donation from the town's most successful lawyer. A local volunteer called to solicit his donation, saying, "Our research shows that even though your annual income is over a million dollars, you do not give one penny to charity! Wouldn't you like to give back to your community through The United Way?"

The lawyer thinks for a moment and says: "First, did your research show that my mother is dying after a long, painful illness and has huge medical bills far beyond her ability to pay?" Embarrassed, the United Way volunteer mumbles, "Uh, no."

"Secondly, that my brother, a disabled veteran, is blind and confined to a wheelchair and is unable to support his wife and six children?" The stricken United Way volunteer begins to stammer an apology but is cut off.

"Thirdly, that my sister's husband died in a dreadful traffic accident," the lawyers voice rising in indignation, "leaving her penniless with a mortgage and three children?" The humiliated United Way volunteer, completely beaten, says simply, "I had no idea."

The lawyer then says "...and if I don't give any money to THEM, why should I give any to you?"

A surgeon, an architect and a lawyer are having a heated barroom discussion concerning which of their professions is actually the oldest profession. The surgeon says: "Surgery IS the oldest profession. God took a rib from Adam to create Eve and you can't go back further than that."
The architect says: "Hold on! In fact, God was the first architect when he created the world out of chaos in 7 days, and you can't go back any further than THAT!"

The lawyer smiles and says: "Gentlemen, Gentlemen...who do you think created the CHAOS??!!"

An old man was on his death bed. He wanted badly to take all his money with him. He called his priest, his doctor and his lawyer to his bedside. "Here's $30,000 cash to be held by each you. I trust you to put this in my coffin when I die so I can take all my money with me."
At the funeral, each man put an envelope in the coffin. Riding away in a limousine, the priest suddenly broke into tears and confessed that he had only put $20,000 into the envelope because he needed $10,000 for a new baptistery. "Well, since we're confiding in each other," said the doctor, "I only put $10,000 in the envelope because we needed a new machine at the hospital which cost $20,000."

The lawyer was aghast. "I'm ashamed of both of you," he exclaimed. "I want it known that when I put my envelope in that coffin, it held my personal check for the full $30,000."

Two lawyers walking through the woods spotted a vicious-looking bear. The first lawyer immediately opened his briefcase, pulled out a pair of sneakers and started putting them on. The second lawyer looked at him and said, "You're crazy! You'll never be able to outrun that bear!"

"I don't have to," the first lawyer calmly replied. "I only have to outrun you."

At the height of a political corruption trial, the prosecuting attorney attacked a witness. "Isn't it true," he bellowed, "that you accepted five thousand dollars to compromise this case?" The witness stared out the window as though he hadn't hear the question. "Isn't it true that you accepted five thousand dollars to compromise this case?" the lawyer repeated. The witness still did not respond. Finally, the judge leaned over and said, "Sir, please answer the question." "Oh," the startled witness said, "I thought he was talking to you."

Two law partners leave their office and go to lunch. In the middle of lunch the junior partner slaps his forehead. "Damn," he says. "I forgot to lock the office safe before we left." His partner replies " What are you worried about? We're both here."

One day, a man is walking along the beach and comes across an odd-looking bottle. Not being one to ignore tradition, he rubs it and, much to his surprise, a genie actually appears. "For releasing me from the bottle, I will grant you three wishes," says the genie.

The man is ecstatic. "But there's a catch," the genie continues. "What catch?" asks the man, eyeing the genie suspiciously. The genie replies, "For each of your wishes, every lawyer in the world will receive

DOUBLE what you ask for." "Hey, I can live with that! No problem!" replies the elated man.

"What is your first wish?" asks the genie. "Well, I've always wanted a Ferrari!" POOF! A Ferrari appears in front of the man. "Now, every lawyer in the world has been given TWO Ferraris," says the genie. "What is your next wish?" "I could really use a million dollars," replies the man, and POOF! One million dollars appears at his feet. "Now every lawyer in the world is TWO million dollars richer," the genie reminds the man. "Well, that's OK, as long as I've got MY million," replies the man.

"And what is your final wish?" asks the genie. The man thinks long and hard, and finally says, "Well, you know, I've always wanted to donate a kidney."

———————————————————————

A teacher instructing on fractions used the following hypothetical with her class: "A man died, leaving behind 20 million dollars. One-tenth is to go to his wife. One-quarter is to be split evenly between his two children. The rest of his money will be donated to charity. What will each person get?" As the students quietly thought about the problem, one raised his hand and answered, "A lawyer!"

———————————————————————

The attorney tells the accused, "I have some good news and some bad news." "What's the bad news?" asks the accused. "The bad news is, your blood is all over the crime scene, and the DNA tests prove you did it." "What's the good news?" "Your cholesterol is 130."

———————————————————————

A lawyer defending a man accused of burglary tried this creative defense: "My client merely inserted his arm into the window and removed a few trifling articles. His arm is not himself, and I fail to see how you can punish the whole individual for an offense committed by his limb." "Well put," the judge replied. "Using your logic, I sentence the defendant's arm to one year's imprisonment. He can accompany it or not, as he chooses." The defendant smiled. With his lawyer's assistance, he detached his artificial limb, laid it on the bench, and walked out.

A defendant who had pleaded guilty saw the jury that had been empaneled, and he announced that he was changing his plea to guilty. When the judge asked why, the defendant pointed to the eight women and four men in the jury box. "When I pleaded 'not guilty,' I didn't know women would be on the jury. Judge, I can't fool even one woman, so I know I can't fool eight of them."

Two lawyers are in a bank when, suddenly, two armed robbers burst in. While one of the robbers takes the money from the tellers, the other lines the customers, including the lawyers, up against a wall and proceeds to take their wallets, watches, and other valuables.

The first lawyer shoves something into the other lawyer's hand. "What is this?" the latter asks without looking. "It's that $100 I owe you."

A man walked into the local Chamber of Commerce of a small town, obviously desperate. Seeing a man at the counter, the stranger asks, "Is there a criminal attorney in town?" To which the man behind the counter immediately quipped, "Yeah, but we can't prove it yet!"

Two lawyers were walking along negotiating a case. "Look," said one, "let's be honest with each other. "Okay, you first," replied the other. That was the end of the discussion.

A personal injury lawyer was on vacation in a small rural town. While walking through the streets, he spotted a car that had just been involved in an accident. As expected, a large crowd gathered. Going by instinct, the attorney was eager to get to the injured, but he couldn't get near the car. Being very clever, he started shouting loudly, "Let me through! Let me through! I am the son of the victim." The crowd made way for him. Lying in front of the car was a donkey.

A millionaire informs his attorney, "I want a stipulation in my will that my wife is to inherit everything, but only if she remarries within six months of my death." "Why such an odd stipulation?" asked the attorney. "Because I want someone to be sorry I died!" came the reply.

"You seem to be in some distress," said the kindly judge to the witness. "Is anything the matter?" "Well, your Honor," said the witness, "I swore to tell the truth, the whole truth and nothing but the truth, but every time I try, some lawyer objects."

A man in an interrogation room says, "I'm not saying a word without my lawyer present." "You are the lawyer," says the policeman. "Exactly, so where's my present?" replies the lawyer.

Mr. Dewey was briefing his client, who was about to testify in his own defense. "You must swear to tell the complete truth. Do you understand?" The client replied that he did. The lawyer then asked, "Do you know what will happen if you don't tell the truth?" The client looked back and said, "I imagine that our side will win."

The New York Times, among other papers, recently published a new Hubble Space Telescope photograph of distant galaxies colliding. Of course, astronomers have had pictures of colliding galaxies for quite some time now, but with the vastly improved resolution provided by the Hubble, you can actually see the lawyers rushing to the scene.

A young lawyer, starting up his private practice, was very anxious to impress potential clients. When he saw the first visitor to his office come through the door, he immediately picked up his phone and spoke into it," I'm sorry, but my caseload is so tremendous that I'm not going to be able to look into your problem for at least a month. I'll have to get back to you then." He then turned to the man who had just walked in, and said, "Now, what can I do for you?" "Nothing," replied the man. "I'm here to hook up your phone."

"I'm beginning to think that my lawyer is too interested in making money." "Why do you say that?" "Listen to this from his bill: 'For waking up at night and thinking about your case: $25.'"

A lawyer, who was talking to his son about entering college, said, "What got into your head that you want to be a doctor instead of lawyer?" "Well, Dad," answered the son, "Did you ever hear anybody get up in a crowd and shout frantically, 'Is there a lawyer in the house?'"

An airliner was having engine trouble, and the pilot instructed the cabin crew to have the passengers take their seats and get prepared for an emergency landing. A few minutes later, the pilot asked the flight attendants if everyone was buckled in and ready. "All set back here, Captain," came the reply. "except for one lawyer who is still going around passing out business cards."

Having just moved to a new home, a young boy meets the boy next door. "Hi, my name is Billy," he says. "What's yours?" "Tommy," replied the other. "My daddy's an accountant," says Billy. "What does your daddy do?" "He's a lawyer," Tommy answers. "Honest?" asks Billy. "No, just the regular kind."

During a party, a doctor is telling a lawyer that he is sick of his friends asking him for free medical advice. The lawyer says, "Just do what I do, and leave a bill in their mailbox." The doctor decides he'll give that a try and thanks his lawyer friend. When the doctor gets home, he has a bill in his mailbox from the lawyer.

A group of dinner guests was blaming all of America's troubles on lawyers when a woman said, "They aren't all so bad. Why, last year a lawyer gave me $1,000." "I don't believe it," the host responded. "It's true, I swear it," said the woman. "I had a complicated personal injury case and what with the lawyer's fee, the cost of expert witnesses, the expense of the appeal and so on, my bill was $41,000. When the judgment only amounted to $40,000, my lawyer simply forgave the difference."

A lawyer passed on and found himself in heaven, but not at all happy with his accommodation. He complained to St. Peter, who told him that his only option was to appeal. The lawyer immediately said that he intended to appeal, but was then told he would be waiting at least three years before his appeal could be heard. The lawyer protested that a three-year wait was ridiculous, but his words fell on deaf ears. The lawyer was then approached by the devil, who told him that he would be able to arrange an appeal to be heard in a few days if the lawyer was willing to change the venue to Hell. When the lawyer asked why appeals could be heard so much sooner in Hell, he was told, "We have all of the judges."

Someone mistakenly left the cages open in the Reptile House at the zoo, and there were snakes slithering all over the place. Frantically, the keeper tried everything but couldn't get the slippery animals back into their cages. Finally, he yelled, "Quick, call a lawyer!" "A lawyer? Why?" "We need someone who speaks their language."

Q: Have you ever heard about taking the Fifth?

A: A fifth of wine?

Q: No, the Fifth Amendment.

Q: What did your sister die of?

A: You would have to ask her. I would be speculating if I told you.

When an 88-year-old mother was called for jury duty, she had to submit to questioning by the opposing lawyers.

"Have you ever dealt with an attorney?" asked the plaintiff's lawyer.

"Yes. I had an attorney write my living trust," she responded.

"And how did that turn out?"

"I don't know," she said. "Ask me when I'm dead."

A thief, a teacher and a lawyer die and when they get to heaven they are stopped by an angel who says, "Sorry, heaven is getting crowded so you need to answer a question correctly before you can get in."

He looks at the teacher and asks, "What was the name of the famous ocean liner that sank after hitting an iceberg?"

"That's easy, " she says. "The Titanic." Having answered the question correctly, the angel lets her into heaven.

The angel turns to the thief and asks, "How many people died on that ship?"

"That's a tough one." the thief answers. "But I saw the movie and it was 1,517." The angel then moves aside to let the thief into heaven.

Finally, the angel turns to face the lawyer and says, "Name them."

Scene: A court room where a person is on trial for murder.

There is strong evidence indicating guilt, however, there is no corpse. In the defense's closing statement the lawyer, knowing that his client is guilty and that it looks like he'll probably be convicted, resorts to a clever trick.

"Ladies and gentlemen of the jury, I have a surprise for you all," the lawyer says as he looks at his watch. "Within 1 minute, the person presumed dead in this case will walk into this court room," he says and he looks toward the courtroom door.

The jury, somewhat stunned, all look on eagerly. A minute passes. Nothing happens. Finally, the lawyer says: "Actually, I made up the previous statement. But you all looked on with anticipation. I, therefore, put it to you that there is reasonable doubt in this case as to whether anyone was killed and insist that you return a verdict of not guilty."

The jury, clearly confused, retires to deliberate. A very few minutes later, the jury returns and a representative pronounces a verdict of guilty.

"But how?' inquires the lawyer. 'You must have had some doubt; I saw all of you stare at the door."

Answers the representative: "Oh, we did look. But your client didn't."

You Need a New Lawyer When...

1. He tells you that his last good case was a "Budweiser".
2. When the prosecutors see who your lawyer is, they high-five each other.
3. The lawyer picks the jury by playing "duck-duck-goose".
4. During the trial you catch him playing his Minecraft.
5. A prison guard is shaving your head.
6. The lawyer places a large "No Refunds" sign on the defense table.
7. Just before the lawyer says "Your Honor," he makes those little quotation marks in the air with his fingers.
8. The sign in front of the law office reads "Practicing Law Since 2:25 P.M."
9. Whenever his objection is overruled, he tells the judge, "Whatever".
10. The lawyer giggles every time he hears the word "briefs".

A small-town prosecuting attorney called his first witness to the stand in a trial – a grandmotherly, elderly woman. He approached her and asked, "Mrs. Jones, do you know me?"

She responded, "Why, yes, I do know you Mr. Williams. I've known you since you were a young boy, and frankly, you've been a big disappointment to me. You lie, cheat on your wife, you manipulate people, and talk about them behind their backs. You think you're a rising big shot when you haven't the brains to realize you never will amount to anything more than a two-bit paper pusher. Yes. I know you."

The lawyer was stunned. Not knowing what else to do, he pointed across the room and asked, "Mrs. Jones, do you know the defense attorney?"

She again replied, "Why, yes, I do. I've known Mr. Bradley since he was a youngster, too. I used to baby-sit him for his parents. And he, too, has been a real disappointment to me. He's lazy, bigoted, and he has a drinking problem. The man can't build a normal relationship with anyone, and his law practice is one of the shoddiest in the entire state. Yes, I know him."

At this point, the judge rapped the courtroom to silence, and called both counselors to the bench. In a very quiet voice, he said with menace, "If either of you asks her if she knows me, you'll be jailed for contempt!"

There was a small jet in mid-flight, carrying a doctor, a lawyer, the Pope, and a small 6-year-old boy (and the pilot, of course). The four passengers were resting in their seats when the pilot came running from the cockpit, saying the plane was having technical difficulties and would soon be crashing. He said, "There are only four parachutes on this plane. I must take one of them, which means one of you must stay on the plane as it goes down…I'm sorry. I'll let you decide how you're going to divide them." The pilot then grabbed a parachute, wished the other passengers good luck, and hopped out of the plane.

The doctor quickly snatched a parachute for himself, saying, "I'm a doctor, and I help millions of people a day. Without me, the world would be full of sickness and incurable diseases." With that, he, too, hopped out of the plane into safety after the pilot.

Next, the lawyer grabbed a parachute, and said, "I'm a lawyer. I deserve a parachute because I am the smartest man alive." After this justification, he leaped out of the plane after the other two.

Now, all that was left was one parachute, and two passengers: the Pope, and the 6-year-old boy. The Pope said to the boy, "Son, I've lived my life, and I'm certain about the fate that will await me when I die. You are so young and have a full life ahead of you. You may take the last parachute."

The boy, amused, simply replied. "Don't worry, Mister. Everything's okay. We've still got two parachutes left for the both of us. The 'smartest man alive' just jumped out of the plane with my backpack."

Last night, a lawyer and his wife were sitting in the living room and the lawyer said to her, "Honey, I never want to live in a vegetative state dependent on some machine and fluids from a bottle. If that ever happens, just pull the plug, OK?"

She nodded, got up, unplugged the TV and threw out his beer.

Once upon a time there was a sheepherder tending his sheep at the edge of a country road in rural Wyoming. A brand-new Jeep Grand Cherokee screeched to a halt next to him. The driver, a young man dressed in a Giogio Armani suit, Stefano Ricci shoes, Ray-Ban glasses, and a Rolex wristwatch, jumped out and asked the herder, "If I guess how many sheep you have, will you give me one of them?"

The herder looked at the young man, then looked at the sprawling herd of grazing sheep and said, "Okay."

The young man parked the SUV, connected his notebook and wireless modem, entered a NASA site, scanned the ground using satellite imagery and a GPS, opened a database and Excel tables filled with algorithms, then printed a 150-page report on his high-tech mini-printer. He turned to the herder and said, "You have exactly 1,586 sheep here."

The herder answered, "Say, you are right. Pick out a sheep."

The young man took one of the animals and put it in the back of his vehicle.

As he was preparing to drive away, the herder looked at him and asked, "Now, if I guess your profession, will you pay me back in kind?"

The young man answered, "Sure."

The herder said immediately, "You are a lawyer."

"Exactly! How did you know?" asked the young man.

"Very simple," replied the herder. "First you came here without being invited. Secondly, you charged me a fee to tell me something I already knew. Thirdly, you do not understand anything about my business, and I'd really like to have my dog back."

An absent-minded attorney rose to defend a client, and intent on winding up the proceedings promptly and reaching the country club, got off on the wrong foot.

"This man on trial, members of the jury," he bumbled, "bears the reputation of being the most unconscionable and depraved scoundrel in the state…"

An assistant whispered frantically, "That's your client you're talking about."

Without one second's hesitation, the lawyer continued smoothly, "…but what outstanding citizen ever lived who has not been vilified and slandered by envious contemporaries?"

A successful and formidable old jurist lingered over the breakfast table reading his *Law Review*, with his wife sitting silently across the table from him–just as she had done every weekday morning for the past thirty-seven years. Seized by a sudden daredevil impulse, she spoke up. "Henry," she said, "is there anything interesting in the *Law Review* this morning?" The jurist frowned and answered gruffly, "Don't be silly!"

The judge frowned when he looked at the defendant and demanded, "Haven't I seen that face of yours before?"

"Indeed, you have, your Honor," said the defendant hopefully. "I gave your son violin lessons last winter."

"Ah, yes," recalled the judge. "Twenty years!"

A browbeating lawyer was demanding that a witness answer a certain question in the negative or affirmative.

"I cannot do it," said the witness. "There are some questions that cannot be answered by a 'yes' or 'no,' as anyone knows."

"I defy you to give an example to the court," thundered the lawyer.

The retort came like a flash: "Are you still beating your wife?"

———————————————————————

A cannibal was walking through the jungle and came upon a restaurant opened by a fellow cannibal.

Feeling somewhat hungry he sat down and looked over the menu...

Broiled Missionary: $10.00

Fried Explorer: $15.00

Baked Attorney: $100.00

The cannibal called the waiter over and asked, "Why such a price difference for the attorney?"

The waiter fetched the cook.....and cook replied, "Have you ever tried to clean one?"

———————————————————————

A man arrested for embezzling millions of dollars went to a criminal lawyer. The lawyer told him, "Don't worry about it– you'll never go to jail with all that money." And, of course, he was right– when the man went to prison, he didn't have a dime!

———————————————————————

A defense lawyer successfully defends a major organized crime figure on charges related to distributing narcotics, murder, attempted murder, racketeering, and extortion. As he is leaving the courtroom for his press conference, an indignant older woman accosts him: "Sir, have you no decency? Is there anyone you wouldn't defend?" Replies the lawyer, "Well, I don't really know…why, what you have done?"

Two friends bumped into each other outside of court one day. "I hear you lost your court case," said one. "Did your lawyer give you bad advice?" "No," replied the other. "He charged me a lot for it."

CHAPTER 10

ONE FINAL HUMOROUS LAWYER STORY

This final humorous story comes with thanks to Shanna Alexander who wrote *The Pizza Connection: Lawyers, Money, Drugs, Mafia* 318-320 (Weidenfeld & Nicholson) (1988). The Pizza Connection case provides a stark example of how a witness's testimony can be exposed as comical if the witness refuses to provide the truthful answers. The Pizza Connection case was a mega-trial involving 18 defendants who were charged with a $1.6 billion heroin smuggling and money laundering that stretched from Brazil to small pizzerias in the Midwest. Trial lasted from October 24, 1985 to March 2, 1987.

The following is Alexander's description of United States Attorney Robert Stewart's cross-examination of an alibi witness, and the cross-examinations a gem of a cross and a hoot:

(Defense counsel) Larry Bronson's defense of (defendant) Sal Greco is focused on his client's need to prove that he was not in a Bagheria farmhouse in early March 1980 watching a heroin quality-control test. Bronson will show he [Greco] was quietly, busily at home in New Jersey. He calls Greco's good friend and tax accountant, Justin Pisano, a man who keeps detailed date books.

Under patient examination by Bronson, the witness goes through a precise account of driving to the Jersey Shore three Sundays in March to go over Greco's accounts and to visit nearby pizzerias with his client in order to compare their business with that of the Greco pizzeria in Neptune City.

Stewart's cross-examination of Pisano becomes this prosecutor's finest hour. He concentrates on the March date-book entries.

"On March 2, yes, I drove down to see Greco," Pisano says, "and we had a leisurely dinner."

"You told us yesterday you were in no rush, right?"

"Yes."

"And that's the truth, the whole truth, and nothing but the truth?"

"Yes."

"Then what is this appointment for 7:00 p.m., with Troviatta?"

"Just a tax appointment. Early March is income tax time, and I made many Sunday and night appointments to service all my tax clients."

"What is Troviatta's first name? Where does he live?"

"I don't remember. I don't even think I do their taxes anymore."

Stewart remembers. He says Pisano was thirty-five miles away from Greco's pizzeria
that night, in the heart of Manhattan, at Lincoln Center, at the opera.

Pisano emphatically denies this. He has only been to Lincoln Center once in his life, to hear Pavarotti.

"Are you an opera fan?"

"Nope. Only been to one opera in my life, when I was in high school."

Stewart shows the witness, and the jury, the Sunday-evening newspaper opera listing for March 2, 1980, at the New York State Theater at Lincoln Center: *La Traviata.* Bronson objects. "Misleading the witness, your Honor. His witness's tax client is named Troviatta—with two t's."

> "And the advertisement for the opera is spelled *T-R-A-V-I-A-T-A*, right?" Stewart asks. "No. It's *La* Traviata," says Pisano gamely.

> "La Traviata?"

> "Right. I don't see the comparison to Troviatta."

> "Except for the time. *That's* a coincidence. Isn't it?"

Pisano agrees, and Stewart directs him to look at the entry for two Sundays ahead,
March 16, at one in the afternoon.

> "Are you referring to Carmen? Carmen Sangari, who I no longer do?"

"Carmen Sangari?" Stewart produces the *New York Times*, and asks him to read aloud the opera listing for that Sunday afternoon. Pisano looks, and agrees that this is truly an amazing coincidence.

Spectators have begun to giggle. But Stewart is not finished. He directs the witness's attention to his diary entry for the following Sunday at 7:00 p.m. "Is that a tax client of yours?"

"The giggling turns to guffaws. The notebook says, "Barber of Seville."

About the Author

Professor Ronald H. Clark is a Distinguished Practitioner in Residence at Seattle University Law School where he has taught Pretrial Advocacy, Trial Advocacy, Essential Lawyering Skills, Visual Litigation and Today's Technology, and Essential Litigation Visuals and Technology.

Professor Clark is a nationally known lecturer and author. He has lectured at over 40 national continuing legal education courses and for numerous bar associations and prosecutor associations across the country. He also has conducted international training for the Department of Justice and Department of State. For 27 years, Professor Clark was in the King County Prosecutor's office in Seattle, Washington, where he served as a Senior Deputy and as the Chief Deputy of the Criminal Division. Next, Professor Clark was the Senior Training Counsel at the National Advocacy Center in Columbia, South Carolina.

Professor Clark has authored over a dozen books including, among others *Pretrial Advocacy* and *Trial Advocacy*; *Jury Selection Handbook; Visual Litigation; Roadways to Justice; Eradicating American "Prosecutor Misconduct"; Powerful Presentations; Trial Advocacy Goes to the Movies, Addressing the Jury. Management and Leadership Handbook,* and *Lawyer Humor Handbook.*

If you are interested in any of the books listed above, you can visit the author's website on Amazon at:

https://www.amazon.com/stores/Ronald-H.-Clark/author/B004AQ8UTI?ref=ap_rdr&store_ref=ap_rdr&isDramIntegrated=true&shoppingPortalEnabled=true

Printed in Great Britain
by Amazon

37233808R00059